T0275142

# A Bit Much

A Bit Much

# A Bit Much

**POEMS**

**LYNDSAY RUSH**

ST. MARTIN'S GRIFFIN
NEW YORK

First published in the United States by St. Martin's Griffin, an imprint of
St. Martin's Publishing Group

A BIT MUCH. Copyright © 2024 by Lyndsay Rush. All rights reserved. Printed in
the United States of America. For information, address St. Martin's Publishing
Group, 120 Broadway, New York, NY 10271.

www.stmartins.com

Design by Meryl Sussman Levavi

The Library of Congress Cataloging-in-Publication Data
is available upon request.

ISBN 978-1-250-32346-0 (trade paperback)
ISBN 978-1-250-32347-7 (ebook)

Our books may be purchased in bulk for promotional, educational,
or business use. Please contact your local bookseller or the
Macmillan Corporate and Premium Sales Department at
1-800-221-7945, extension 5442, or by email at
MacmillanSpecialMarkets@macmillan.com.

First Edition: 2024

5   7   9   10   8   6   4

*For Michelle Pfeiffer*
*(You know why.)*

# Contents

## PART II

## When the Monster Turns Out to Be Three Dogs in a Trench Coat

# PART III

## When You Have Main Character Syndrome and Aren't Looking for a Cure

The quality of life is in proportion, always, to the capacity for delight. The capacity for delight is the gift of paying attention.

JULIA CAMERON

# Introduction

This is a book about fun and feelings and, occasionally, potato chips. I knew from a very young age that I was a bit much, but it took me a long time before I realized what a gift that is. I hope my poems reveal, remind, or convince you of that, too. I also hope they make you laugh. (Duh.) And cry. And feel powerful and cute and tender and astonished and invincible. True to my truth, I organized this collection by mood and emotion so that you can always find what you need, when you need it, including an entire section dedicated to cheering for yourself. You're welcome and I love you.

Legend has it that I didn't start writing poems until the hot, young age of thirty-seven and even then, I only began to dabble once I discovered that for me, a poem is simply a joke with an epilogue. That, of course, is the origin story of @maryolivers drunkcousin, which is, in turn, the origin story of this real-life book of poems you're now holding in your hands. Thank you for reading. I'm (we're all) so lucky you're here.

# A Bit Much

# PART I

# When You Have a Crush on Everything and Everyone

TYPE

## LOVE LETTERS

CURRENT OR DESIRED MOOD

### bubbly, besotted, astonished, optimistic

# In Florida, an Invasive Snail Is Helping Save an Endangered Bird

*NPR, March 14, 2023*

In Nashville, an artist is designing a T-shirt that says,
"Legalize Drag Brunch," and in Minnesota a bill is being passed
that will provide free breakfast and lunch for all students
All the way across town, a man is making a point to
shut down his friend's sexist joke and just over yonder a woman is
taking her senior dog out in a stroller so he can see and be seen
Right this very minute, someone, somewhere, is
       holding the door open for a stranger
       conceding the parking space
       calling their mom back
       letting love override their long-held beliefs
It's true that goodness is an endangered species
but it survives
in a shell
on a shirt;
invasive and relentless once it catches the light

# Make Like a Tree and Love

Scientists have a hunch that
trees can become dear friends
      Linking roots to swap resources
      Bending branches back to share sunlight
      Shielding each other from the wind
Most of what I know about love boils down to this
simple distinction:
Who stays, and who
      leaves

# Tonight I'm Doordashing

Cacio e pepe (it won't travel well, but I always try) / chicken potstickers with soy ginger dipping sauce / a smashburger from Cafe Roze / fries with ranch / one (1) day at our family cabin that my parents sold in 1999 when the divorce was final / a large tortilla soup from Mas Tacos / two beef arepas with sweet plantains and creamy cilantro sauce / a Cherry Coke Zero / the sound of my mom laughing at my joke / the feeling of holding my nephew Jack minutes after he was born / a wood-fired pepperoni pizza with hot honey / a chocolate malt (not a milkshake, how dare you) / the way he said, "I love you" for the first time as if it were a prayer / yeah, you can just leave it at the door / I'll be right there.

# Someone to Eat Chips With

All I'm looking for
is someone to
Laugh at all my jokes
Give me the pickle that
comes with their sandwich
Explain Daylight Saving Time to me
every year (multiple times)
Read the entire contract and
tell me if I should sign
Bear the weight of my failures
but be the first to put a feather in my cap
Be the keeper of my heart
and the curator of my secrets
Stand in the dark doorway of
our uncertain future
and step inside
Is that so much to ask?

# Safe Travels

We're in the car heading to the airport and my three-year-old niece is sad to see me go. So sad, in fact, that she has hyper-focused on a bag of safety equipment that's in the trunk; "You need to take it in case of emewgancy, Lulu," she insists, on repeat. I say *okay, baby,* but what I'm actually tucking away in my overhead compartment (my brain, duh) isn't a red bag with a white cross / It's the tight coils of her golden curls / her expressive eyebrows / how at certain moments she reminds me so much of my brother I could cry / You see, I know from experience—having lived far from family my entire adult life—that it's memories exactly like this that I reach for in times of trouble / it's memories exactly like this that keep me safe and sound.

# Frequent Crier

I'm at the airport and I'm falling in love with everyone: The octogenarian rolling a pink duffle bag with white polka dots / The woman I heard on the phone saying, "Well, we put Mom's funeral on my credit card, so it might be maxed out," / The adult man who ordered apple juice—with his whole chest—as his in-flight beverage / The young couple in my row who were as gentle with each other as they were with their newborn / It seems as though I have been twitterpated / as though this turbulent, communal experience has become an altar for my faith in humanity / I'm up in the air / and on my knees / believing that everyone is doing their best / that we're actually looking out for each other / that maybe the mess we've made of things is redeemable after all / and then / the wheels touch the tarmac / the seatbelt sign goes off / and the deplaning process brings me right back down to earth.

# I Think My Parents Invented the Staycation

In 1991
In a Hilton in downtown Minneapolis
About an hour away from our house
and our horses
and our standard weekend night playing Uno

Tell me anything more exhilarating
than sprinting down a long, carpeted hall
to the vending machine
*Girls, watch where you're going!*

Show me a finer dining experience
than sitting on a fancy hotel bed eating pizza
Imagine a greater thrill than an indoor swimming pool
while it's below zero outside
Conjure up a luxury that beats falling asleep to
a pay-per-view movie

It's incredible they'd go to all of that trouble
when they couldn't even Instagram it

# Be  st
# Fri  ends

I send you a rambling voice note about how maybe I should try a different shade of brow tint this time / a little lighter / not so harsh / what do you think? / You know the passcode to my phone / and the name of that one guy I met on Bumble who cried about the movie *Groundhog Day* / and how much it hurt to leave Chicago / We've lost hours plotting paint colors / text replies / outfits / trips / what will happen on the next *Insecure* / what to do with our lives / "why are men?!" / who to trust / when to let go / You're a soft place to land / a hard, wheezing laugh / the closest I'll come to another sister / I used to think all of this in-between stuff was the intermission / the rest stops along the way / the amuse-bouche / the filler flowers / but lately I've come to realize that all of this small stuff *is* the stuff / this is it / the main event / the blue plate special / a million little drops of love that fill the whole cup.

# Code Red

A great philosopher once said
*I saw the sign and it opened*
*up my eyes (I saw the sign)*
But when you see the world
through rose-colored glasses
It can be hard to recognize
a red flag
So what I have learned is this:
If they're mean to the waiter, they'll be mean to you
If they never follow through, they will never show up
If it hurts your stomach, it will hurt your heart
You can't temper a storm
But you can sure as hell evacuate the beach

# Crush Energy

I used to be worried
that I would only want
love that I couldn't have
That the mere fact of it being
available to me
would make it repulsive;
Not wanting to be a member
of any club that would have me
etc., etc.
Maybe it was therapy,
maybe it was fate or dumb luck
but with you
the adrenaline I felt
wasn't because I knew you'd leave
it was because I knew you'd stay

# You've Got Mail

*Acts of service* is not my love language. My mother tongue is eye contact, a tender word; gourmet sandwiches. But for the last five days I have witnessed a man pull up to my neighbor's driveway, unload his supplies, get out his folding chair, and continue the patient work of building her an elaborate, brick mailbox. My elderly neighbor Norma is—to put it in the unfussy way she did when she showed up on our doorstep the day we moved in—dying. Now, I'm not sure if the man building the mailbox is her friend or her brother or her lover, but you don't have to look too closely to see that his work is fueled by something much deeper than money. And as the day passes, brick by brick, and the sun gets higher in the sky, I think of all the forms I've seen love take—open arms, open doors; gourmet sandwiches— and I add a new one to the list: mailboxes.

## How to Talk Dirty to Me

Reply to one out of every three texts I send you
Dodge my questions and plans
Give me your wishiest-washiest emotions
Make my head spin and
Hang me out to dry
Stain my memories with faded colors and
white lies
This is an endless cycle and as much as we
rinse and repeat
only one of us ever feels clean

# Love Is What, Now?

Sorry, you lost me at love is "patient"
Kind? No prob
Trusting, hopeful, persevering?
Bing, bang, boom
It's just that first one that gets me
We both remember when
we were in line for bagels and I remarked,
"I can be patient . . . just not for long,"
to which you wryly replied, "Pretty
sure that doesn't count as patience."
But joke's on you because
it's quite "1 Corinthians 13" of me
that I had no trouble whatsoever
waiting my whole life
to find you

## Loving Each Otter

Hold my drink
I have something cute
to say to the group:
Otters hold hands while they sleep
Wait, there's more!
They do it to protect themselves
from prey
and to make sure their loved ones
don't float away mid-snoozle
I hope that the love you find
and the love you give
keeps you safe
in this swirling sea

## What a Catch

Back when my attachment style was
Velcro
I did not hate the player nor the game
In fact, I was usually in the front row
of the bleachers—
Cheering on men who played the field
Admiring their athleticism as they dodged commitment
Timing how fast they could run circles around my boundaries
I saw myself on the Kiss Cam;
a fangirl available to everyone but herself
who didn't seem to care at all
that the match never ended in her favor

# We're Not Getting Any Younger, Woman

*After "Firstborn" by Nicolle Galyon*

And god, isn't it fantastic? How our best qualities have been barrel-aged / ready for harvest / splashing into half-full glasses / and staining our lips the perfect shade of red? / How we've tempered and tended our tendencies / left it all on the field / on the page / and how our best-laid, five-year plans went awry? Isn't it a splendor to see what's been growing while we've been growing / older / even when the self-care instructions were completely ignored / and the elements were all wrong? Is it not a marvel that we're letting ourselves go / right over the hill / hands in the air / and managing to enjoy the ride / and the view / and the detours? Pretty miraculous, if you ask me, how after all these years the only thing we've truly lost is our "give a shit" / and our cool / and the ability to successfully evade a hangover / Admire, for a moment, how the years are teaching us that we don't need to "bounce back" / or "age gracefully" / or keep up with anything but the good work / I used to believe my best was behind me—best shot, best days, best body / but that got old / and so did I / In fact, if there's one piece of ancient wisdom I've learned as a dinosaur born in the late 1900s / it's that / plans are like foreheads / wrinkles make them a lot more interesting.

# Like Trying to Hold a Snowflake

Sometimes when I am distracted
and you've just done a sweet thing
or said a tender word
And I didn't give it my full attention
I wish to go back
to three seconds ago
so I can grab the moment
as it falls
and make sure
its magic soaks into
my skin

## You're the Only Ten I See

Right around the time
the world went south
So did I
Yep, in the Terrible, Horrible,
No Good, Very Bad Year of 2020
I left Chicago for Nashville—a reverse pilgrimage
that I did for love
          almost blindly;
my heart driving me down I-65
away from one true north
towards another
And there are many mornings I look around
and feel like a stranger in someone else's backyard
But then my vagabond heart reminds me that
sometimes home isn't a place
it's a person

## My Boyfriend Is From Alabama

Today I learned that pecans fall from trees when they're ripe
and the best way to crack them open
is to take two and squeeze them together in your hand—
the pressure of the closeness
exposing the good stuff
Is that a nice metaphor for relationships?
His aunt says, *Masks may not help*
*but they certainly can't hurt*
I guess when your mama's mama and her mama
grew up on the same street,
maybe it's not as much closed minded
but close minded—a bunch of pecans
that fell from the same tree
His mother insists that she has never said a single swear word
in her life
Meanwhile, my go-to exclamation is an ungodly combo that
would bring her to her knees
I'm writing this in my head, in the shower, in the home where
my boyfriend was quite literally born and raised
The water begins to cool so I shift my mind back to the task at hand
I wash the rest of my body and
my mouth with soap

## This Little Light

Too late to turn back now
I already said the quiet part
out loud
You can't have been surprised
We both know I give off
Big "Says *I Love You* First" Energy
But when the night is this dark
and full of terrors
I don't want you to wonder
how I feel
I don't want to hide it
under a bushel (no!)
I want my eager face
to set you at ease,
unmoored as we both may be

# Until the Snow Begins to Fall

I look at you across the room
and I see
Golden days
I see years
that were icy and blue
for reasons we can't quite recall
I see my home for all seasons
I see the many, strange ways
that you do your best for love
And I'm awash with
all the tender sweetness
I simply cannot hold

## Ante Hero

We fell in love the way I eat Doritos
slowly and then all at once
At the risk of sounding like someone
who gets misty eyed and insists,
*When you know, you know*
I'll say this: I've never been lucky
when it comes to love
But with him
it didn't feel like a gamble at all
to put all of my chips on the table

## This 500-Ton Boulder in Finland Has Been Balancing on Top of Another Rock for at Least 8,000 Years

*Good News, May 9, 2023*

Look, babe, it's me and you
Or to be grammatically correct:
      you and me
I strive, like that sentence structure,
to put you first
and every day I watch you do the same—
      *Here, have mine. No, you sit. I ordered your favorite.*
—those tiny pebbles of affection leaving a ripple effect
So although our history is not yet ancient
This fight against nature
is exactly what keeps us
rock steady

## Covered

You say "You're covered in dog hair," like it's a bad thing
Turns out I am also covered in
long strands of my own hair
Doritos dust
The blood of Jesus Christ
when my mother prays for me
I try to cover myself
in gratitude
to ward off what it feels like
when someone on Instagram gets something that I want
Regularly, I find "I love you impossibly" written
on my to-do list in my boyfriend's handwriting
and it covers my entire body
like a soft blanket
Remember Snuggies?
Unconditional love is a blanket with arms

## Dawn Soap and a Toothbrush

Sometimes I get worried that life will out-life us / That the everyday misdemeanors we commit against each other will turn us into frenemies / or worse: roommates / You, standing when you eat / Me, never shutting a cupboard or drawer / Us, subconsciously keeping track / keeping score / even though winning almost always feels like losing / The jeweler showed us how to clean the engagement ring / reminding us that the setting is delicate and we should be gentle with it / Fuck me up if that isn't great relationship advice: Regularly scrub the record / Polish the parts that have tarnished / Handle each other with care.

## All of the Awkward Things I Missed
## During the Pandemic

Not knowing what to say to the dressing room attendant
when handing them back the truckload of jeans that didn't
"work" / Hugs where both of you turn your heads in the
same direction so you're sort of doing the tango / *"Have
a good flight!" "You too!"* / Uber Pool / Trying to eat a
passed app from atop a cocktail napkin when one hand is
preoccupied with a glass of champagne / Sending over-
medium eggs back when the yolk isn't runny / Belabored
small talk with a new hairstylist / Being goofy with small
children who are staring at you from the grocery cart seat /
Walking back to the group after your turn bowling / Clunky
high fives at a sports bar with someone in the right
jersey / The pedicurist looking at your heel and getting out
the big daddy file without saying a word / Shuffling past
people in your theater row to go to the bathroom / When
social distancing became the new normal, my introvert
mask started to slip / and I came to the reluctant
realization that maybe / the communal rhythms of cringe
/ aren't so much the epidemic / but the cure.

## These Are the Days

When my pants barely fit and
I fall asleep every night at 7:45 P.M.
When I entered my Donut Era and
started wearing a bra to bed
When you won't let me carry anything and
the dog refuses to leave my side
These are the days when everyone will tell us about
the long days
and the short years
and how we should sleep while they sleep
and cherish every moment because they grow up so fast
These are the days of Big Opinions and long lists of must-haves
and stacks of books we will never read
And on days like these
      when we manage to focus on
        the only day we're promised (today)
we can't believe our luck
that these days are even ours
in the first place

# Caretaking Notes

Thanks again for watching our special gal / she's at such a fun age, so this should be a breeze / Let's see / there's plenty of food in the fridge / but she will look at it all and suggest Postmates / this is fine / life is short and / the bag of lettuce has already gone bad / We try and limit screen time / but, again / life is short and / she's learned a surprising amount of useful things from TikTok / Getting her to bed at a reasonable time is a herculean—yet vital—task / this means you may have to try and talk her out of that 3:30 P.M. cup of coffee / She will fight you on this, but / remain firm and if necessary / remind her how much she loves sleep / There's emergency cash in the drawer / in case you two discover a new skincare line or / loungewear set / or fancy snack brand / We'll be back first thing tomorrow morning but / don't hesitate to call or triple text if you need anything / Remember: her big feelings are completely normal for her developmental stage / she's just a young little thing / she's only 39 years old.

# Hand Me Downs

Her middle name / His last / Her eyelashes / His strong legs / The memory of those years on the farm / and at the cabin / and church after church after church / The diamonds her mom wore in her ears / the signet ring with Gramps' initials / The vagabond excitement of moving / on / and starting / over / Men who leave / men who stay / women who do too much / and harden because of it / In the 90s when your parents got divorced, people referred to your home as broken / *"She comes from a broken home,"* they'd say / and I'll give you one guess which group of people were the most critical of those fractures / (hint: it was neither atheists nor agnostics) / But while they were busy keeping score / we were counting our blessings / we were piecing back together what was lost / I know now that it will never add up to them / but that makes it all the sweeter to me / because it's mine / it's ours / and love like this is always a winning game.

## Mortifying Every Poet Dead
## and Alive by Trying to Describe Love

Love is a heated towel
Fresh sheets
A blanket with arms
Love is a perfectly timed inside joke
The first firefly of the summer
Having your hair braided
Puppy breath
Love is getting dressed for dinner after a long day at the beach
    Damp hair
    Sunkissed shoulders
    Soft linen
    The faint smell of sunscreen and orange blossom
Love is rounding the bend on a darkened road
seeing the porch light on
and realizing you finally found your way
home

# PART II

# When the Monster Turns Out to Be Three Dogs in a Trench Coat

TYPE

**EPIPHANIES**

CURRENT OR DESIRED MOOD

**inquisitive, impassioned, gobsmacked, riled up**

# His Body Is Bread and so Is Mine

It is bonkers
that someone made up the term
"problem area"
And we were all like,
*Oh yes I have those*
*and they \*do\* seem up to no good*
*now that you mention it!*
The gospel I was raised on
told me my soul was born broken
So I guess it should come as no surprise that
I believed without question
that my body needed saving too

# Hysterical

I'm going off the deep end
anyone want anything?
I'm in the market for some
deep, cleansing screams
A few meditative complaints
A mantra or two made up entirely
of curse words
Do they make a "Rage Spiral" scented essential oil?
How about a "Worst Case Scenario" flavored
herbal tea?
Sounds delicious and insane
pour me a double
I crank up my "Unhinged Hits" playlist
and relax into my hissy fit
If anyone needs me for the next 2 hours
I'll be just down the road
losing my mind

## Things That Taste as Good as Skinny Feels

Boxed brownies with homemade icing / an ice-cold, West Coast IPA / letting *I love you* roll off of my tongue / and meaning it / queso / butter / cream cheese / knowing that the way my body looks is the least interesting thing about me / @GrossyPelosi's Vodka Sawce / Krazy Jane's Mixed-Up Salt / buying jeans that fit / compliments that are unrelated to weight loss / kind words I speak to myself / Whatchamacallit candy bars / smashburgers / nearly every flavor of potato chip / the comfort that I am "pulling it off" simply by putting it on my body / BLTs / Spicy Nacho Doritos / not regurgitating the dogma that I was force-fed as a kid / tomatoes straight from the garden / a New York–style bagel / body neutrality / wearing shorts again / fountain Cherry Coke / unfollowing accounts online that perpetuate diet culture / or make me feel weird about the body I live in / what a gorgeous spread / I think I'll go back for seconds.

# It's All Downhill After 30

Sheesh, tell me about it! It's a *rapid* decline
Like the back road in your hometown
that you cruised your bike down on a dare
      Wind in your face
      Tears in your eyes
Downhill like where lush valleys reside
offering shade and reflection and rest
Downhill as in ambling towards ease, pleasure, joy
Downhill like an exhale
a soft landing
a Slinky's descent
Yes, that's exactly what growing older feels like,
if you're down for the ride

## Hot Sh*t

I really felt it when Mindy Kaling said
that people feel uncomfortable
around women
who don't hate themselves
Because
I don't think I'm hot shit
but I do think I'm, like, warm shit
An editor would cut that line
but I'm going to keep it
I'm sick of diluting myself
just to be palatable

## Love Yourself, Gurl!

Body positivity is fantastic / for everyone else / Me? I still have big dreams / of smaller limbs / "Long, lean muscles" like my Pilates instructor promises / Ballet arms like my barre teacher guarantees / I knit in my ribs and pull my belly button into my spine / I activate my glutes / I squeeze my shoulder blades together / *Don't forget to breathe!* / When my little sister was 11 / She listed this in her New Year's Resolutions: "Get a four-pack" / On the one hand this is devastating / On the other, I appreciate the realism / six-pack abs? No, thanks, just a four-pack should do! / If I were a man I would be really proud of these strong legs.

# I'm Giving Up for Lent

What would it feel like to give up
      self-improvement
for forty days?
Would the tightness in our chests
throat, shoulders, and hips
ease as we contentedly took the easy way out?
Would capitalism crumble if we deleted our wish lists
and framed the before photo?
Sounds holy, if you ask me,
to be sold on life as-is
to just exist
with only this, only us
only what these two arms can hold

## Reverse Aging *The Easy Way!*

Dress head to toe in your favorite color / come up with a secret handshake / ask someone to cut your sandwich into triangles / no crust! / make some imaginary friends / buy a pair of Rollerblades / draw a stick figure portrait of your family / hide something under your bed / write in your diary / eat more pizza / scream in delight / get a goldfish and name him something like The Fish Prince of Bowl-Air / perfect a few knock-knock jokes / and magic tricks / and at least one weird thing you can do with your joints/eyeballs/tongue / love like no one's watching / dance like everyone is / hunt for four-leaf clovers / get lost in a daydream / stay out after curfew / make a grand gesture to your crush / tell everyone who is mean to you that they're not invited to your birthday party / or that your dad can beat up theirs / or that you are rubber and they are glue / place glow in the dark stars on your bedroom ceiling / next to a poster of a celebrity heartthrob / across from your inflatable dELiA*s chair / sing yourself to sleep / relax into the truth that there are no monsters in the closet / that fun is never a waste of time / and maybe—just maybe—a life of joy will be your greatest achievement.

# Let Go and Let Goddess

"She really let herself go,"
Um, don't threaten me
with a good time
I would love to spend
the rest of my days
letting myself
go free
go bananas
go off
Sounds amazing actually
to release my grip on
what anyone else wants
from me

# Abs of Steel, Buns of Cinnamon

is the real title of a book collection of *Cathy* cartoons
The artist behind them, Cathy Lee Guisewite,
said her work centers around what she called
the "four basic guilt groups" of a woman's life—
        food, love, family, and work
I'm not sure if Cathy (the writer) was lampooning
or normalizing this distinctly feminine shame
but I know there's big money in the business of
convincing women we are always failing at something
"Aack!" on us, that we'd put something as grave as that
in the funny papers

# Wet n Wild Geese

*After Mary Oliver*

You do not have to be good
at makeup.
You do not have to walk on your knees
for a hundred miles through a Sephora, repenting.
You only have to let the soft contours of your face
look how it looks.

## Growing a Pair

Around 1851, women were regularly put in jail
for wearing pants
All they wanted was to get in on the practicality of the trouser
but men were like,
IN YOUR DREAMS, DOLLFACE!!!
WE'RE THROWIN' YOU IN THE SLAMMER!!
Which is so embarrassing for them—
to be threatened by a pair of slacks
Silly boys,
we were always going to find a way to wear the pants
(see what I did there?)
Maybe, as a way to honor these women
      who fought hard for equality so I could have the right
      to complain about low-rise coming back,
I'll buy some jeans that fit

# Wrong Answers Only

Wow so embarrassing
all this time I thought
photographers instructed us to say "cheese"
because cheese makes people happy
I thought "shop small" meant buy a dollhouse
and "good in bed" meant how much
of your day you spend tucked in there
I thought the most important duty
of my life was to not give the milk away for free
and I thought feeling fearful was
a core part of being faithful
I thought being wrong was the worst thing I could be
But I was wrong
See? Look at that: not so scary after all

## Basically an Archaeologist

Today I learned that TIL means
today I learned
There is so much
I don't know
and I can only partially
blame Christian schooling
(Don't get them started on dinosaurs!!)
It took me almost 24 years to discover
that new information is not a threat
it's a gift
What would happen
if we recognized doubt
as a sign of faith?

# Mermaid in America

Sometimes I don't recognize my own knees
in photographs
Probably because for years I hid my legs under
maxi dresses / party pants / strategic poses
anything to skirt attention
from what I had determined was my
most troublesome area
I always thought Ariel was one dinglehopper short of a full grotto
for wanting a pair of these
Hadn't anyone told her about the scrutiny
the comparison / the cellulite / the Spanx /
the cankles / the saddlebags?
I'm mostly over it now, but that's only because
where I live it's way too hot
to hate yourself out of wearing shorts

# Boo!

The spookiest haunted house
I've ever been to
is an evangelical church:
Everyone hides behind a mask
There's at least one main ghost
And the entire thing hinges on
a bloodbath
Wouldn't you also be scared
if you were taught that
you are powerless
to save yourself?

## Abs-olutely Hysterical

It's October of 2020
and all I have left are upper abs;
the very tippy top of a six-pack
I used to work very hard on my body
but this year I've had to work very hard
on my mind
If comedy is tragedy + time
maybe one day we will laugh
about all of this
so hard our abs hurt—
all two of them

## Maybe Crocs Are Okay

Compression workout leggings are over
You heard it here first
This fall we are wrapping ourselves
in cloud-soft clothing
We are cocooning up
in marshmallow materials
We're floating about town looking like
the dancing inflatable outside of a car dealership
We are allowing our bodies to breathe
our bellies to exhale
our feet to land softly
If you happen to see me in a huge coat
it's probably just my down comforter
I have officially lost interest in
the business of constricting myself

## Prime Time

The year is 2022 and I'm searching
"bandana top" on Amazon
I wore one twenty-some years ago
in the prime of my life
and now everything from the 90s is back
in style, except:
Leaving your phone in your purse
for the entire house party
Looking people in the eye, and
spray butter
(I feel okay about that last one)
We didn't have Amazon Prime back then
and we were still happy
(Weren't we?)
My new going out top will arrive tomorrow
because I've decided that
      I'm in my prime
for as long as I say so

# A Race Against the Guac

Society tells women
that we are avocados;
ripe for just the teensiest amount of time
*Better make guacamole while you can!*
Then—faster than you can say,
"Guac is extra"—we're seen as
bruised, gray mush; too soft to be useful
But joke's on them:
we've been queso this whole time
And ask anyone
that shit never gets old

# Goops I Did It Again

I'm going to let you in on a li'l secret:
The fourth step in my
morning skincare routine is
screaming
> Step 1: cleanse
> Step 2: vitamin C serum
> Step 3: hyaluronic acid
> Step 4: a guttural, feral scream
> Step 5: moisturizer
> Step 6: sunscreen

This simple regimen is my key to
radiant, glowing skin
and I'm certain even Gwyneth would agree:
Before you let the sunshine in
you have to let the rage out

## Help

The Matron Saint Anne Lamott
taught me
that the three essential prayers are
Help
Thanks
Wow
If you're feeling weird lately
it's probably because we've spent
nearly three years
stuck
on that first one

## "You Have a Lot on Your Plate"

Omg thank you for noticing
I *do* have a lot on my plate right now:
Between work and hobbies and relationships
and the stack of books I look at lovingly every night
while I open my phone to scroll TikTok instead . . .
Not to mention the steaming-garbage state of the world!
My proverbial plate is absolutely overflowing
with important work and worries and dreams
Isn't it a miracle I'm this lovely?
Anyway, what's new with you? And before you answer,
could you please pass the rolls?

# Ordering from the Kids' Menu

I hope I never take myself so seriously / that I stop thinking it's funny to pretend that one of those giant pretzel rods is a cigar / I hope I never forget to put Bugles (and olives) on the tips of each of my fingers / or to eat a Nutty Buddy one layer at a time / or to carefully pull each strand of string cheese until it's gone / I hope I keep suggesting to "Lady and the Tramp" a long spaghetti noodle until someone says yes / I hope I never stop squirting Reddi-wip directly into my mouth / spearing a single macaroni noodle onto each tine of my fork / and attempting to eat popcorn by throwing it straight into the air / I hope I always fill each tiny square of my waffle to the brim with syrup / and blow bubbles in my chocolate milk / and assemble my two eggs and bacon into a breakfast-plate-smiley-face / and pretend the banana is ringing with an important phone call I must take right this minute / I hope when I'm 83 years old I find myself using a cookie cutter to turn my sandwiches into fun shapes / Even though I'm no longer young / Even though they tried all my life to convince me that / play / was something I ought to outgrow.

# A Chip off the Old Narcissist

I used to regularly fight with my dad
over potato chips
True story, he used to call me "Chip Vac"
as in vacuum
Wouldn't you also argue with a man
who called you that?
Wouldn't you rage against
the suggestion
that you should deny your hunger?
Wouldn't you tell him
that the only thing that sucks
is how
he's never looked at you
and not seen everything he hates
about your mother
The air in the room is gone
and so are the chips

# How Lovely to Be a Woman

*I am good,* you declare
        over and over
        every day
through exclamation-marked emails
endcapped LOLs
and $0.77 apologies
*I am good,* you insist
hoping to earn even a fraction of
what is automatically given to men
Bad men, even
Bad men, especially
        over and over
        every day

## Promise Ring Pop

Dodgeball
Foosball
Pizza & Mountain Dew
That's what the boys did
while we were given
"the talk" about purity
Ya know, the one that
distilled women down to either
an object of desire or a threat
The one that told us that
it's our job not to tempt anyone
The one that said virginity is
our most valuable gift—
and no one wants a regifted woman
Thinking back on it gives me
an ache in my ribs
right where they told us
we came from

# Keep It Simple, Susan

When I hold the word *success* under a blacklight
what glows back at me is *ease* and *freedom*
        Not Scrooge-McDuck-esque vaults of swimmable gold
        Not clout or fame or for The Joneses to eat my dust
Just 9–10 hours of sleep
Work that feels like play
And terms and conditions that I write myself
Joy does not have to be an end-of-year bonus
or something we squeeze in during PTO
The other day I learned that one of our senses is called
*chronoception*
It means, the ability to feel the passing of time
And I do
        I really do
And one of my proudest accomplishments
is that I don't need a vacation
from my vacation

## "Marie! The Baguettes, Hurry Up!"

Whether we like it or not, some things take time: intricate pastries, building credit, Zoom meetings, balayage / but there's a laundry list of things that simply can't wait (laundry, for the record, not being one of them) / big things like speaking your truth / making the move / taking the break / setting yourself free / and not-so-big things like signing up to help / or remembering a name / or looking someone in the eye / One thing Taylor Swift and I have in common / is last names full of urgency / so take it from us / and remember that, of all the things you should never postpone / make sure joy is at the top of the list.

## Heck Yes, I Have an MFA: Major Freakin' Attitude

I don't want to teach poetry
Not to you
Not even to me
I do not want to scrutinize the words or
hold the sentiments upside down by their ankles
to see what shakes out
I don't want to know what my body of work
could have or
should have become
It's a body, after all—it lives and it breathes and it fucks
things up constantly
And sure, I may never wrap my head around
most of what I wrap my tongue around
But that's ok: I don't write the rules
I just write poems

# Beware of Lost Boys

For years and years I dated men
(first red flag, amirite?)
who were drawn to my bright light
but ultimately wanted to put me in a jar
for their own ambiance
*Ahh, much better,* they thought, *a soft, subdued glow all to myself*
Eventually they were faced with the dark truth
that reveals itself to all dim men:
Fireflies and Tinker Bells like me
will flicker out entirely
if our magic is only reserved
for the nonbelievers

# Double Duty

Eating for two
Going on long walks for two
Choking down giant prenatal vitamins for two
Reading a new version of the same headline every week
with semi-automatic numbness
for two
Grieving for two
Darkly laughing at the phrase "pro-life" for two
Mapping out exits for two
Scanning crowds for suspicious behavior for two
Metabolizing that the same people who would've made me
bring you into this world against my will
don't care what could take you out of it
        for two

# There Are No Exceptions for the Life of the Mother

The state I live in does not
really care about my life
So I eat chips for breakfast
Hold my hand to my chest
Feel my steady heartbeat and
attempt to digest how
all it would take
is
a few, new, tiny cells
to make that hearty thud
a complete afterthought

# A Republican in Sheep's Clothing

There will always be those who get their fill
from sinking their teeth into anyone
who is different from them
We may not be able to convince them
how sick their hunger is
But we can sure as shit help
protect those they're
hunting

# Resurrectile Dysfunction

In 2013 I could no longer get it up
    my spirits
    or my faith
The only solution, as I saw it, was to lie
down (I've always been very good in bed)
So I did exactly that; subsisting on wine and bread
until the stench of decaying dogma dissipated entirely
When I was ready to resurrect
I revealed myself to the women first
They listened to my story
Took account of my scars
Proclaimed me new again—reborn, some might say
And when asked about my life-saving miracle;
my *un*-salvation
Their report was simple:
She hath risen
She hath risen, indeed

## Mum's the Word

For the first 12 weeks we held our tongue
Then for the next 8 we held our breath
Everywhere in between—and certainly afterwards—
there has been a constant stream of words
of advice
of delight
of warning
My dental hygienist asks if I'm planning on breastfeeding
My mother-in-law recounts her complicated labor and delivery
My mom friends near and far tell me to enjoy my sleep now, and
to kiss my old body goodbye
The first time the baby has hiccups in utero, I panic-google,
"Fetus in distress?!"
And all I can think about some days (when I am not thinking about cake)
is how my husband moves through the world
Invisibly a dad-to-be
Blissfully sipping on a half-full beer while not a single soul asks him
what crib he's registered for

## Retirement Plans

Next time you feel like you're late to the game / or you've missed the boat / your moment / your shot / I hope you think of 88-year-old Johanna Quaas, the oldest active gymnast in the world / and Harriette Thompson / who ran her first marathon at 76 . . . and her 15th at 91 / On all of the days you're certain that you're too old / and it's too late / I hope Sister Madonna Buder comes racing across your mind / the same way she has in the 45 Ironmans (and counting) she has under her belt (habit?) at 92 / And if that doesn't work, I hope the image of Nola Ochs accepting her bachelor's degree at 95, and her master's at 98 jolts you from your despondency / or that you google the oldest newlyweds in *The Guinness Book of World Records* and learn about George and Doreen Kirby who married at 103 and 91, respectively. Of course, you don't have to become the oldest woman in the world to reach the summit of Mount Everest, like 76-year-old Tamae Watanabe / or the most senior person to jump out of a plane like Dorothy Hoffner did when she was 104. But you do have to own your becoming / You do have to have the courage to begin again / and again / and again / You do have to accept that defying the odds is not just for triathletes and Nobel Peace Prize winners / it's for people like you / and people like me / people like World War II veteran Patricia Davies who began hormone therapy at the age of 90, so that she could spend every second she had left making herself proud.

# PART III

# When You Have Main Character Syndrome and Aren't Looking for a Cure

TYPE

## CHEERS & FIGHT SONGS

CURRENT OR DESIRED MOOD

**present, self-assured, loud, proud**

## She's a Bit Much

You mean like a bonus french fry in the bottom of the bag? Like a champagne shower? Like triple texting good news? Like buying coffee for the person behind you in line? Or did you mean "a bit much" like an unexpected upgrade to business class / or theme parties / or the band pretending to go off stage and then coming back for an unforgettable encore? Perhaps you were referring to that thing of being astonished by a sunset / or how puppies flop around when they learn to run / or the way some people take karaoke really seriously? Maybe you just meant sprinkles / confetti / balloon drops / witty comebacks / generous tips / fireworks / waterslides / serotonin / cherries on top / and the fact that maybe we were put on this planet simply to enjoy ourselves? Then yes, I agree—she *is* a bit much. Aren't we so lucky she's here?

## Hot Girl Walks

Have been happening since the dawn of time:
>Through fields
>To the well
>Down darkened hallways
>With signs raised above heads
>In lockstep
>In cahoots
>One foot in front of the other
>Away from danger and
>towards it, too
History (forgive me, *herstory*) has
been changed, and made, and
cured and broken
by women all over the world doing
the hottest thing imaginable:
walking
each other home

## Cool as a Cucumber

I am not the type of person one would call
"composed"
I'm generous with my laughter
It doesn't take much to make me cry
And my temper has no trouble going kablooey
It may not seem very cool
or collected
but the way I see it,
life is full
of so much hardship
we may as well let what comes easy
come easy

# A Little Bit Louder Now

Be the silly straw you wish to see in the world / Be a bouncy house / A spork / A chilly day driving with the windows down and the heat on / Be one of those deep sea, glow-in-the-dark creatures that have only been photographed once / Be curly fries / Be a hat with a spinning top / Or a comically oversized sun visor / Be Silly Putty / Silly String / The silliest goose in the gaggle / An enormous cloud of cotton candy / Be bright purple lipstick / A dog in a stroller / The least-sexy costume at the party / The wave at a hockey game / A flower growing out of a crack in the concrete / Be a platter of sizzling fajitas / A balloon drop / Ten gaudy fingers of insane nail art / The hokey pokey / Caps lock / A fun riddle for the whole table to guess / Be a song on repeat / An elaborate, secret handshake / An inside joke vanity plate / A sparkly pantsuit / A wheezing laugh / Fried chicken on a waffle / Be exactly what you thought you weren't allowed to be / Be it big / With no end in sight / And put your whole butt into it / Make no sense and / Make no apologies / Pop out of your life every day like it's a giant cake / We don't need you to play it cool / We don't need you to dial it back / We're just so happy to have you.

# A Little Bit Louder Now: The Remix

you re allowed to
be big And
Make no apologies

You're allowed to be
big
and make no apologies

## Shedonism

I pour myself an iced coffee
to take in the car on the way
to go buy an iced coffee
You see, I'm trying to squeeze pleasure
into as many cracks in my day as I can
(How one spends their cracks
is how they spend their life, no?)
It's the same reason I chose a career
where I do not need to set an alarm clock
Cock-a-doodle-doo? I don't know her
A few years ago Kim Cattrall famously said
"I don't want to be in a situation
for even an hour where
I'm not enjoying myself."
And I have no edits; just awe and admiration
that she's clearly stopped attending
bridal and baby showers

# An Idiom-Proof Life

If you're looking for someone who has all of her ducks in a row
maybe try one house over?
As you can see, all I have are these silly geese
and I mostly just let them fly
      by the seat of their pants
      too close to the sun
      in the face of decorum and expectations
If you're looking for my eggs, though,
they're usually all in one basket (I prefer full-ass to half, *thank you*)
If I'm in the mood, I'll strike while the iron's hot
but most of the time I like to let the grass grow under my feet,
keep my nose safely away from the grindstone,
and play my life like a great piece of jazz:
fast and loose

## It's Called Maximalism, Babe

Why shouldn't I stop and smell the espresso beans / Or say, in a voice a little too loud, *This is the best margarita I've ever had!!* / Or use the full curse word / Or have my dessert first? / Why shouldn't I give it my all / And do it for the story / And leap before looking / And let love consume me? / Why shouldn't I use my expensive face creams with abandon / Triple text my crush / Laugh at my own jokes / Cry at commercials / Sing at the top of my lungs while I vacuum / Buy the orange chair / Paint the town purple / And fly across the country for the weekend just to pinch a cheek? / Why shouldn't I hold your face in both of my hands at 11:30 A.M. on a Tuesday while you're chopping a salad and remind you that you're the center of my happiest days? / Why shouldn't I memorize how the sun comes in from the front window / Turn the music up / Give the dog a piece of cheese / Say what I mean / Let my hair down / Forgive fast / Believe that the best is yet to come? / Tell me—no really—why shouldn't I? / Why shouldn't we? / Why shouldn't you?

# It's Called Maximalism, Babe: The Remix

Why shouldn't I ▬▬▬▬▬▬▬▬
▬▬▬▬▬▬▬▬▬▬▬▬▬
▬▬▬▬▬▬▬▬▬▬▬▬▬
▬▬▬▬▬▬▬▬▬▬▬▬▬
▬▬▬▬▬▬▬ let love consume me ▬▬
▬▬▬▬▬▬▬▬▬▬▬▬▬
▬▬▬▬▬▬▬▬▬▬▬▬▬
▬▬▬▬▬▬▬▬▬▬▬▬▬
▬▬▬▬▬▬▬▬▬ And ▬▬▬
▬▬▬▬▬▬▬▬▬▬▬▬▬
▬▬▬ hold you ▬ in ▬▬▬▬
▬▬▬▬▬▬▬▬▬▬▬▬▬
▬▬▬ the center of my happiest days? ▬▬
I ▬▬▬▬▬▬▬▬▬▬▬
▬▬▬▬▬▬▬▬▬▬▬▬▬
▬▬▬▬▬▬▬▬▬▬ Believe that
the best is yet to come ▬▬▬▬—no really ▬ why shouldn't
I? ▬▬▬▬▬ Why shouldn't you?

Why shouldn't I
let love consume me
and
hold you in the center
of my happiest days?
I believe that the best is yet to come
—No really
Why shouldn't I?
          Why shouldn't you?

# And the Oscar Goes To

FYI if you ever see me make a typo
it's just because I'm a method actress
trying to understand what it feels like
to be average and relatable
This also goes for when I
—Walked face-first into some hanging branches
because I was looking at my phone
—Honked aggressively at a car only to realize
it was empty, parked, and I was in the wrong lane
—Pronounced "banal" like "anal"
And especially that time I yelled, "Birk nation!"
to a girl who was wearing
the same Birkenstock sandals as me
If you witness me doing things like this
all you need to do is
report back to my acting coach
and tell her that I am absolutely
crushing it

## Braggadocious with the Mostess

High on my own supply?
Thanks for noticing!
Turns out—while illegal in most states—
Self-Love is a helluva drug
(if you can get your hands on some)
I know it would make the world
a lot more comfortable
if women continued to hate themselves
But I tried that for years and
I'm bored out of my mind

## "What Have You Been Up to Lately?"

Oh, not much / Just making a fool of myself / Making a name for myself / Making the most of myself / Making it up as I go / Making a leap of faith / Making my bed every morning / Making myself clear / Making a fuss / Ya know, the usual / I've actually really gotten into making a mountain out of a molehill / Making a face / Making an entrance / Making it rain / Making it happen / Making up for lost time / Making tacos for dinner / Making sure he knows just how much I adore him / Let's see . . . on the weekends I've been making a break for it / Making a game of it / Making a night of it / Making a big deal / Making my best guess / Making my own luck / Making a short story long / Making your day / Making mine / I've really been trying to prioritize making a scene / Making it interesting / Making it count / Making a comeback / Making a difference / Making a mess of things / Making the best of things / Making tiny, beautiful things I'll be proud to leave behind / Yeah that's pretty much it over here—how about you?

# Peace, Not Quiet

The meanest thing
anyone can say to me is "calm down"
(A close second and third being
"that wasn't funny,"
and "the snacks are gone.")
I'm not here for a quiet time I'm here
for a resounding one
I'm here to grate fresh parm all over my life
and never say "when"
I'm here to grab life by the clown nose
and squeeze
I've made it a sacred practice to speak
my mind and
my daily breathwork is laughter
So perhaps I'm living proof that
you don't have to pipe down at all
to find inner peace

## Drinking Iced Coffee in January

I suspect the reason we got so hyped
when our parents would make
breakfast for dinner (!!!)
was because our tiny spirits could already sense
how intent the world was on smooshing us
into predictability;
how the whole damn thing seemed to hinge on
following protocol
how heavy it felt to plan way in advance
for delight
It didn't take me very long to learn that I like my eggs
and my life a little more scrambled than that

# The Results Are in, Amigo, What's Left to Ponder?

What if we woke up today and bit off more than we could chew just to remember what it feels like to be satiated / What if we got reacquainted with our tastes / Fed the beast / Starved the fever / Ate our hearts out / What if we danced with our demons / Fought with the devil / Sat with the darkness / Made our own light / What if we sent the DM / Told the truth / Stopped apologizing / Bought jeans that fit / Spiked the punch / Put the song on repeat / What if we raised our hand / Asked the hard question / Gave that belief system a hearty nudge right in the ribs to see if it flinches / What if we let the grudge go / Let that person go / Let ourselves go / Tried something new / Yucked it up / Fucked it up / Shrugged our shoulders and tried one more time / What if we winked in the mirror / Flirted with disaster / Chalked it up to fate / Stole another glance / Lost our cool / Went back for seconds / What if we left it all on the field / Played our hearts out / Emptied the tank / Saw it through / Closed down the bar / Went down swinging / What if we stopped with the numbing / Felt all our feelings / And lived to tell the tale / What if the questions are more important than the answers / What if we've known the truth all along / What if none of it matters / What if all of it does?

# (I've Had) the Maritime of My Life

I'd love to chat with the inventor of the waterbed
I feel like we'd have a lot in common
Or, at the very least, a shared belief that
filling everyday monotony with whimsy
is our only chance at
Saving Our Souls
Tonight, I'll drift off to sleep;
my thoughts buoyed by how
much better my life has become
now that I've decided to spend it
making waves
instead of holding my breath

## Share Plates

*Of course* I'd like seconds / and a refill / and at least one dessert that's partially on fire / Have you tried this life lately? / Not the one on the sandwich board (work, errands, emails) / The one on the secret menu / with specials like Playing Hooky, Starting Over, Taking the Leap, and Whooping It Up / The one where the soup du jour is happy tears / seven days a week / and the only sides available are fries and flamboyance / There's no need to worry about sharing, either / it's all served family style which means there's plenty to go around (they recommend anywhere from seven to thirty-six tapas per table) / So, someone get me one of those lobster bibs / I'm about to honor my hunger / I'm about to bite off more than I can chew / I'm about to make a huge mess.

# An Error Message Just for You

You are not a Roomba
or Rosey from *The Jetsons*
or Pac-Man or Inspector Gadget or
a Tesla with a vanity plate
(they all have vanity plates)
You're more Florence than Machine
More holy mother than motherboard
Here for much more than to be user friendly
So take this as a reminder—flashing on the screen in yellows and reds—
to power down
and let your systems process
Because even an optimus in her prime
such as you
is not designed to constantly operate
at full capacity

# Every Little Thing She Does Is Magic

So we throw her an elaborate surprise party for her job promotion
        (all of her friends and family fly in for the occasion)
We meet with jewelers to design a delicate gold ring
for her second anniversary with therapy
We create a multi-store gift registry for how she learned to
set boundaries with her mother
We schedule a golden hour photoshoot of her and her new apartment
And we buy her a "push present" for deciding she does not want children
We plan an all-inclusive vacation to celebrate her deepest friendships
(the outfits will be *incredible*)
We host a five-course dinner complete with effusive toasts
for finishing her graduate program / doula training / yoga certification
We place a crown on her head and wrap a hot pink boa around her neck
in garish jubilation for the life she is building
brick by brick
by and for herself

## The FBI Agent Watching Me Through My MacBook Camera Knows

My mirror face / how long it actually takes me to do my nail art / all of the times I eat dinner directly from the pan I cooked it in / the way we greet the dog with hyperbolic razzle-dazzle even though all the books say not to / By now they've noted the look in my eyes when I come up with the punchline for a poem / the volume you have the game at every Saturday / and Sunday / and sometimes Monday night / how often we write things we've already done on our to-do lists just to cross something off / I hope, amidst their routine cataloging, they've learned a few things too / like how important it is to cry it out / how you don't have to know all the words to the song to sing along / how good it feels to forgive / how love is somehow fireproof and fragile at the same time / And if most of that is too hard to make out from the tiny camera / I hope they're at least enjoying all of my attempts at yoga handstands.

# It's Amateur Hour Somewhere

Starting something new
is like a one-man show
for a one-man audience:
the only applause worth seeking
is your own
Don't rob yourself of that
while you wait for approval
from somewhere else
Sometimes winning yourself over
is the greatest show on earth

## Two Very Enthusiastic Thumbs Up

Today I will be my own best critic / I will give myself 5 stars just for showing up / I will notice every nuanced effort and fine touch / I will applaud the debut performances of new talents / or habits / I will rave about the pacing, the blocking, the lighting, the writing / I will exclaim that this is the best life I've ever tasted / I will close my eyes and chew slowly / I'll give compliments to the chef / and the director / and the artist / and the muse / (me, me, me, and also me) / I will dub myself the voice of a generation / ahead of my time / reinventing the genre / blazing a new trail / a savant / "who knows what she'll think of next!" / I will insist that everyone see the show / at least once / if not twice / there's not a bad seat in the house / I will write up the review nicely / unlimited word count / no edits / post it in the Sunday *Times* / 10 out of 10 would be me again.

# Two Very Enthusiastic Thumbs Up: The Remix

Today I will applaud
this life
And
compliment myself
at least once, if not twice
      There's no limit

# A Spell for Success

Unplug your computer
But—wait!
Don't start it back up again
Delete your social accounts
But—first!
Pick a house off of @cheapoldhouses and buy it
Now pack up all of your favorite
things and people
and drive off into the sunset
Perhaps you will take up tap dancing
or learn to bee keep
Could be that you're a natural at knitting
or writing thrillers
Maybe you will spend your days
making jars and jars of homemade jam
and the sweet aroma of doing something
just for you
will smell exactly like
success

## Almond Joys

Sometimes all it takes to let joy in
is a little reframing
Don't believe me? Just watch:
It's not a vending machine,
it's an arcade game
you always win

# Cartwheeling Snakes May Be Trying to Bamboozle Predators

*IFL Science, April 5, 2023*

The dwarf reed snake clearly knows
what some of us know all too well:
that the best defense against our enemies is
a little razzle-dazzle
It's to our advantage that haters are repelled by
joy
So we armor ourselves tits-to-toe in body glitter
We bring confetti poppers to a knife fight
We decorate our resilience and resistance with every color of the rainbow
We disorient those who wish us ill by being louder, prouder
      a bit much
And if you're thinking, "How can a snake do a cartwheel
without arms or legs?"
Well, 1) That's the language of the oppressor
2) That's showbiz, baby, and
3) You just fell right into our trap

## She's So Sensitive

Dude, I know! It's almost like she opened her eyes and her arms and her pores to all the tender mercies and undertones of this screwball world / and let it soak all the way in / Like she missed class the day they talked about playing it cool / and having a poker face / and keeping your heart way, way off your sleeve / Sorta seems like she's made the unpopular decision to be astonished / affected / a mess / and not clean it up before the guests come over / It's as though she's feeling her way through a thinking world / and making us watch / our tongue / our step / how we move through life / how it moves through us / I see what you mean, though / it's a lot to take in— for anyone who prefers their senses to be sensible / And if it weren't such a dazzling sight / I'd look away too.

## She's So Sensitive: The Remix

She opened her eyes
to this screwball world
and made the unpopular decision
not to look away

## Good for Her

How liberating to know
that your success
doesn't detract from
the likelihood of mine
and vice versa
We don't have to be envious
or discouraged
Success is a pie with unlimited pieces
And the scarcity we fear
is just an old wives' tale
I mean, look at Dermot Mulroney
and Dylan McDermott:
They basically have the same name
and they're doing just fine

## Strong Female Lead

Billy Shakes said that all the world's a stage. So when people gripe about Main Character Syndrome, I'm like, IDK, take it up with the boss. I'm too busy romanticizing this one, juicy little life I have on this tiny, spinning rock to worry about the optics. I hear music in surround sound when I walk around the neighborhood or try on new clothes in front of the mirror. I rewrite every awkward moment as a meet-cute. I feel awash in a warm spotlight when I say something clever. I take off my wedding ring before a workout and pretend I'm melodramatically leaving my philandering husband, Richard. I imagine a talent scout spotting me at the grocery store and saying, "That gal's got somethin'!" I am a triple threat (singing, joking, snacking) and I am putting on the performance of a lifetime—line by line, day by day. And the voice yelling "Encore!" from the cheap seats just so happens to be mine.

# Have We Met Before?

The only thing the pandemic gave back to me
was my own face
I guess when the world is on fire
one tends to stop reaching for mascara
When all hell breaks loose
you sorta lose the itch to
yassify yourself with Instagram filters
It's three years later and
I still don't like what I see in the world (most days)
but
most days
I like who I see winking back at me
in the mirror

# Hard Pass

On days when my silly little humor piece
gets rejected
again
When the client wants something a little
safer
when
everyone online is funnier, smarter
hotter, Going Places
I take a deep breath and listen to
the swish swish of the dishwasher
the dog chomping on his food
you singing off key in the kitchen
my own tender heart beating
And remind myself that
all of this is art too

# 2 Hard 2 Pass: Director's Cut Ending

(And when that doesn't work
I write the world's most scathing
email
questioning their taste
defending my genius
rejecting their rejection
and for some reason insulting
their haircut?
And then with the truly heroic self-restraint
my adoring fans and critics love me for
I delete
before sending)

## 2023 and Me

Whoever you're itching to become,
     start now
Pretty sure Big Calendar made up
when the year starts
so why not make up
for lost time and consider today
your new year
(new you)
Most rules are just suggestions, after all, and
if pleather can successfully rebrand as
Vegan Leather™ you can be
whatever you want

# Like a Duck Eating Lunch

Face down, ass up
that's the way I like to
focus
on my own path
my own plot
my own personal chart-toppers
I don't want to be so distracted by
how everyone else is
working the crowd
that I forget to honor
the strange little song
only I can sing

## She's Not a Serious Artist

It's almost a joke, honestly,
how she spends all of her time playing
    with words
    with fire
    to the crowd
Last I checked, she was entirely unconcerned with decorum
or formalities or precedent;
preferring to make up the rules as she goes
and then refusing to refer to them as rules at all
She seems to have spent her entire career
counting peace and pleasure as benchmarks of success, and
letting lighthearted breezes carry her
into rooms she has no right to be in
What a farce, what a laugh—
she almost had us convinced that the truth
doesn't have to hurt in order to heal

# I Am Not Afraid to Be Seen Trying

Or changing my mind
or getting it wrong
or freestyling instead of learning the routine
I'm not afraid of self-promotion
or making a big deal out of it
or patting myself on the ass
I'm not afraid of low like counts or pissing off the algorithm or content that flops
And I'm not afraid to be cringe, or extra, or A Bit Much™
Sure, there are things I'm scared of—like sharks and blond beards and
talking to strangers on the phone—
but of all the monsters under my bed,
the only thing I truly fear
is letting fear get in between
me
       and anything I really want

# For She's a Jolly Good Fellow

For the last two years I have been celebrated
within an inch of my life:
a wedding
a house
a baby
a book deal
Leave it to me to cram a large hunk of major life moments
into the sunset years of my 30s
But I have no regrets
 . . . except for how funny I feel with all of the
beautiful brouhaha showered down on me in such rapid succession
        the parties the toasts the gifts—jeezus, the gifts
I sound ungrateful, I know, but that's not it
I'm proud and weepy and enamored and astonished
I just can't figure out how to make sure we bake cakes and
buy trick candles and make slideshows and leave comments full of confetti emojis
for all of the milestones that have nothing to do with boys or babies
I don't have the answers
but when I blow out my birthday candles next month
I think that's what I'll wish for

## Out of Office Message

Thanks for your email! SIKE—the only emails any of us are actually thankful for are ones that tell us our package is arriving today, our food is almost here, or that we landed the gig. If your message does not fit into one of those categories, please consider me out of the office, out of reach, out of my mind, and out of patience. I will be far, far away from my inbox until the phrase "Can I pick your brain?" is outlawed or we find a way to convince clients that their edits always make the piece worse—whichever comes first. If your request is urgent, no it isn't. If you can't figure it out without me, yes you can. If you *really* can't figure it out without me, aren't you grateful I'm so talented? Let's make sure to circle back on that when I get back to you next week/month/decade. Thanks in advance, xoxo.

P.S. Your email found me well because it did not find me.

# PART IV

# When Someone Telling You to Relax Actually Works

TYPE

## LULLABIES

CURRENT OR DESIRED MOOD

**tender, turbulent, anxious, wistful**

# BREAKING NEWS: Local Woman Gets Out of Bed

We're getting reports that
an area woman has yet again
done the impossible
That's right, Ken, sources have confirmed
that she opened her eyes, took a deep breath
and stepped out into the day
to face the many strange and delightful horrors
that the world keeps in its back pocket
Look how she faces the sun
Look what she's making of the mess
Look what's become of her bravery

# Reassurances to Save for a Rainy Day

No one is mad at you. No one thinks you're stupid. (Honestly, everyone thinks you're hot.) No one noticed that one embarrassing thing you did back there and if they did, they already stopped thinking about it. You're doing a great job. You look cute today. You are very funny. You would be missed. It's okay. Things happen. You will get another chance. Everyone you admire has had to ask for help. If they left, they are not the one. If they made you feel small, they are not the one. If they tip 10%, they are not the one. What you're feeling is totally normal. That person was wrong about you. You can pull that off (maybe reexamine the idea of only wearing clothing that is "flattering"— it's maybe not the guiding light it should be). There's nothing to be ashamed of. Things will get easier. You are not in the way. What you're feeling makes sense. You do not have to earn joy or rest. You do not have to be your "best self" every day. (And if someone tells you this they are a life coach trying to funnel you into a six-week course. Run.) No one does it like you. It is not too late. You are not too old. You are worthy of good things. If cauliflower can be pasta you can be whatever you want.

# Cracks of Light

I'm so grateful that
bad days are often followed
by good ones
That sometimes while it's raining
the sun makes a little cameo
That time really does heal
and in the meantime, sleep helps
That our dogs can tell when we
need extra comfort
That when the worst case scenario
takes us by surprise
so does our own strength

# I'm Not Like Other Girls, I'm Worse

I am a little tugboat that runs
on affirmation and approval
Toot toot! Look at me go!
Did you see me go just then?
Cute, huh?
I can do it again if you'd like!
Here's an important fact
about tugboats like me:
We may be surprisingly strong
But deep down in our hulls
all we want is
to be handled with care

# Cute, if True

That penguins mate for life
That red wine is good for the heart
That you can help a friend who has been stung
by a jellyfish simply by peeing on them
Cute, if true, that the alignment of the planets and stars
on the day we were born determined our personalities
That dogs sneeze for attention
That Einstein failed math
That you held out hope for us for over 7 years
before sending that message
Cute, if true, that everything happens for a reason
That there's a life after this one where we can all be together
That tomorrow is our chance at a clean slate; a fresh start,
and no one other than us has been keeping score after all

# Sweet Dreams (Are Made of This)

When I go to sleep at night
I count all of the Nicolas Cage movies
I can name by heart
I count the ideal number of
chocolate chips in a cookie (eleven) and
I count up to twenty in Spanish (brag)

I count the times I said no;
prioritizing my boundaries over politeness
And the times I said yes;
prioritizing hope over fear
I count the number of freckles on your shoulder
and all the days since I first started counting them
I count every time I laughed;
with double points for the times
I made my own self laugh

I tally up all of my wins
so I can beat the part of my brain
that holds the sum of my losses
at its own game

## About 500 Pounds of Pasta Was Found Along a Stream in New Jersey

*USA Today, May 5, 2023*

And you think *your* dreams are too big?
Too strange?
Too (forgive me) *impastable*?
If a quarter ton of noodles can swim upstream
so can you
If spaghetti and macaroni and ziti can beat the odds
they're not alone
And if this unexplained, carby miracle
puts a fire in your belly to follow your whimsy
down to the river for a nonsensical feast
You don't need to think too long or hard about it
You just have to bring a fork
      You just have to show up hungry

## A Hump Day Blessing

Don't let an Instagram quote make you feel guilty
about your level of productivity
You may have as many hours in the day as Beyoncé
but that is where the similarities end
(To be fair, I have not seen you dance, I'm just guessing)
Whatever does not get done today will get done eventually
or it won't
which means it was never that important in the first place
Being busy is not a personality
and you do not have to turn every hobby into a "side hustle"
Please remember that rest is not Self Care™
it is a basic necessity
No one can drink from an empty well

## Sticky Notes

There are a few reminders
that keep me afloat
One: even positive change can be hard
Two: certainty isn't the end goal of faith
Three: my physical appearance is
the least interesting thing about me
These are my mental pool toys
and yes
one is shaped like a pizza

# I Can't Imagine a More Beautiful Thing

I'm done aching for peonies in October
and blackberries in February
I will eat corn on the cob in the height
of harvest;
enjoy every last kernel
And when the winter rolls around
I will remember how some things
are always in season
including me

## Easy, Breezy, Lemon Squeezy

Today I am untouchable. Like I am some mob boss's daughter. Like I am a castle surrounded by a piranha-filled moat. Like I am rubber and you are glue and whatever you say bounces off me and sticks to you. Today, my feathers cannot be ruffled, my cool cannot be lost, and I cannot be bothered. My jaw and my butt cheeks are unclenched and, in fact, every muscle in my body is as pliable as a Slinky. (I do a few back walkovers on my way to get a Topo Chico from the fridge—just for fun.) Today I observe the chaos around me without feeling solely responsible to fix it. I tilt my head to the side with an almost-amused grin when things don't go as planned. I am not in a rush, in a panic, in the way, or incapable. I am the zen-iest zen to ever zen. I am focused on the here and now and if you ask me about the past or the future I will say something like, "Hush now, sugar, the present is a present." (I will sound exactly like Matthew McConaughey in that moment and it will soothe us both.) Today I am not walking, I'm floating. I am not chasing, I'm receiving. I am not holding on, I'm letting go. I am silk running through fingers, a butterfly's kiss, water off of a duck's back—so light, so unworried, so calm even the gentlest breeze is jealous.

# Easy, Breezy, Lemon Squeezy: The Remix

Just for fun, I grin
when things don't go as planned
I am here, now
like the unworried, gentle breeze

## Stillness and Silliness

almost look like the same word
And maybe that's because
they both ask you
to let go
and have the courage
to be at home with yourself

## There Are Dozens of Us

Maybe it will provide a little comfort if we can acknowledge the tiny humiliations that we all experience regularly: Like, looking back accusingly at the jagged piece of sidewalk we just tripped on / Waving at someone who was certainly waving at the person behind us / The final seconds of a Zoom call / Never knowing what to say when someone knocks on the single stall public restroom we are currently inhabiting / Googling ourselves / Admitting we were wrong / Asking for help / Giving our hearts away / We're cavemen with computers in our pockets / What did we expect?

# That's Why They Call It Eco *Friendly*

No act of kindness is ever wasted
I have it on good authority that
every last bit of compassion is recycled
and remade
into another useful item
or composted and
used as soil to plant a tree
that provides shade
and a place to rest
and a sturdy trunk to lean one's head against
This is dangerously close to becoming
Shel Silverstein fan fiction
But you catch my drift:
We need whatever you have
to give
even if it's just a damn

# When Are You Guys Gonna Have Kids?

99 percent of the time the only person who can
tell me what to do is myself or my dog
But I am willing to make a rare, one-time-only offer
for anyone who can tell me
definitively
        whether or not to have children
No, not your personal opinion
or your best guess
or your thoughts on climate change
I'm simply looking for someone able to peer
far into the future and report back exactly
which tine of the fork I should follow
Which "what if?" will haunt me more gently
Which loss I will be able to bear
Act now! This deal
(and most of my eggs)
expires at midnight

# The Darkest Day of the Year

Sorry but LOL that we keep thinking
it can't get any darker out there
And then, like the surprise party
you insisted you did not want,
more bad news pops out of a cake
I'm not above taking something
as a good omen, though, so
if winter solstice means that tomorrow
will be brighter
and the next day, brighter still
I will take solace—
as we slowly inch towards the sun—
that perhaps the worst is behind us;
shivering in our shadow

## Celebrate Bad Times . . . Come On!

The last two years have been cloudy with a chance of what the fuck / So we're celebrating every win, no matter how tiny: Sending a hard email / Flossing / Running the seven-minute errand that has been haunting your to-do list for three months / Saying no / Saying yes / Getting through the day without setting something on fire / Let me check my notes— yep! That calls for a standing ovation / A bucket of Gatorade over the head / A fireworks display / A touchdown dance / A flowery, teary acceptance speech thanking your agent (you) and your manager (also you) / Because at times like this / in a world like ours / even the most subtle sign of forward motion / counts / Even the slightest hint of good fortune feels like a home run.

## If I Don't Text Back

It's just that I got caught in a doomscroll
spiral / became unraveled by a Twitter
thread / opened up a can of worms and a
can of whoopass / fell down a YouTube
rabbit hole and did not find wonderland /
took the red pill and chased it with
champagne / sent a few rage-DMs / rubbed
a magic lamp but only Christina Aguilera
appeared / fell asleep between a rock and
a hard place / then waded into hot water /
threw my phone in the ocean / watched it
drift away like an ominous message in a
bottle / What did I miss? / Was it all a dream /
or is the world still on fire?

## Today, Let's Harness the Confidence of a White Man Jaywalking

No rush
No little, apologetic jog;
Just the unrepentant bliss
of getting from where we are
to where we need to be

## A Get-Together to Fall Apart

You're cordially invited to my pity party. It's gonna be a blast! We're complaining about the slightest inconveniences. We're pouting about the hand we've been dealt. We're ranting about the state of the world and making a mood board of every random, offhand thing anyone has ever said that hurt our feelings. When we're done with that we'll play a few rounds of Mall Madness (that thing where you numb the pain by buying something online that you don't need), prank call our exes, and freeze someone's bra. Then we'll go to bed angry in our *NSYNC sleeping bags and finally—for one sweet night—let our bitch faces rest.

# Top Down, Cruising in My Own Lane

I slip the *Do Not Disturb* sign
onto the doorknob of my life
I've got important work to do:
Minding my own business
Accommodating my whims
Guarding my joy;
nose buried in the story
      only I can tell

# Advice to My Younger Sel—LOL JK No

If given the chance to pay a ghostly-ass visit
to my younger self, I'd be tempted
to impart some wisdom to her, like:
—the importance of learning to laugh at yourself
—or a reminder that the shape of your body is not a problem to be fixed
—or how the secret to swallowing vitamins is to tip your head down
(which is super counterintuitive)
But I'm a pretty firm believer that
making mistakes is what makes us
So I'd save my spooky breath except for this one, crucial
revelation that could save Young Me
twenty or so years of turmoil:
sensitivity isn't a weakness
it's a superpower

## Reassurances to Save for a Stormy Day

You are a brave little toaster. And you make really fantastic toast. (Honestly, people would pay big bucks for just a single slice.) You will get through this. It won't be this painful forever. You are stronger than you think—and I'm sorry you have to be. It's okay to need help. It's even okayer to ask for it. You made the right call. This is the thing that is leading to the next right thing. If it does not serve or sustain you, you can let it go. What is for you will not rest until it finds you. Tomorrow will be better. And if not tomorrow, then the day after. Maybe the day after that day, max. The world would not be the same without you. We're on pins and needles to see what you come up with next. We're so lucky to have you. You're so lucky to have you. If bananas can be ice cream, you can be whatever you want.

# Eye Creams & IRAs

Being in your mid-30s means
Sharing antidotes for back pain
Planning happy hour at least two (okay, three) weeks out
Discussing the merits of kitchen appliances
with unironic passion
But it also means
Wearing my personality
like a favorite sweater
Taking "she's a bit much" as a compliment
Seeing glimmers of wholeness emerge from
years of inner excavation
And finally understanding how taxes work
JK I'll get to that when I'm 60

# How Do You Kiss Your Old Body Goodbye?

Like a crush? Curious, sloppy, urgent?
Or, more like a lover? Deep, passionate, pleading?
Perhaps, with a hint of irony, you kiss your old body goodbye
like a mother: soft, protective, prudent—
aware with instinctive certainty that
most endings
are simply beginnings
in disguise

# Siri, Play "Peaches" by Justin Bieber

I bruise like a peach
Low iron, clumsiness, genetics?
IDK, probably all three
When my husband and I
were dating long distance
I would send him photo updates
of my random bruises
and call it Bruise News
I hope you're as proud
of your sensitivity
as I am of mine

## You Can't Please Everyone

And this, Honeybun, is fantastic news
I spent decades juggling and tap-dancing
with a hula hoop around my waist
and bells on my ankles
and a soft smize on my lips
But then, as a bit, I stopped diluting my feelings
into watered-down crowd-pleasers
And instead, served myself up
as a complex, tart, funky delicacy—
an ice-cold quencher appreciated only by
those with excellent taste

## To Anyone Who Saw Me Walking Down Riverside Crying

Listen. I was just listening—to a Canadian composer playing the piano for my morning soundtrack / to myself whispering to the cherry blossoms that last night was the last of the frost. *I promise.* I was simply struck by the familiar sight of those church doors / and the relief that I never have to walk through them / or into any small (minded) rooms that believe they get to decide what love is / and who it's (not) for. *Never again, amen.* And then, just where the road starts to curve, I found myself admiring the dog's springy trot while I did the math on how many morning walks we have left together (don't worry, he will defy science and live to be 100). So, yeah, those weren't happy tears that you saw, nor were they sad; just a mix of ache and hope and seasonal allergies.

## I'll Hold It for You

The worry you store neatly in your ribs
The breath you haven't let out since 2020
The world that's perched on your shoulders
The love that might tear you in two
I know you're the type of person who
hates taking more than one trip
to bring in the groceries
But
That looks heavy—
give it to me for a minute
I'll hold it for you

# I Will Remind You of Your Joy

Of the softer side of the memory
The immeasurable love that defined the loss
The small pleasures still waiting to greet you
I will cool your face with hope and
bear your sorrow while you sleep and
hang a banner on your door that says,
      laughter is not a betrayal
I know there is no bright side to this grief
But
Let me open the curtain for you just a smidge—
I swear I can almost see a break in the clouds

# California to See Its First Superblooms in Years

*The Wall Street Journal, April 4, 2023*

If you, too, have been waiting since 2019
to enter your Spectacle Era,
the Golden Poppies, Whispering Bells, and Milkmaids
have some great news to share:
The drought is over
The heavy winter rains have come and gone
And those hillsides that you thought would never blossom again
are about to be covered in tennis-ball-sized
bursts of orange and yellow
        So vibrant they'll draw a crowd
        So bright they can be seen from space

# Wild Goose Chase

When your surroundings begin to feel cold and
      uninhabitable
and your environment no longer offers
the support or sustenance you need
      I hope you migrate
I hope, as you make your way south,
that you find other silly geese to fly with, too—
in such a tight-knit formation that Wikipedia
would refer to your crew as a *plump*
And I hope that no matter how long the journey takes you,
the wind is always at your back; nudging you closer to
      home

# What It Feels Like to Be at Peace with Myself

There are at least four, tall, tasty beverages in front of me / the voices in my head are singing in three-part harmony / and the intrusive thoughts that pop up are just fun facts about 90s sitcom stars / My limbs are "inflatable dancer at a car dealership" loose / but my spine is strong and straight / I see a candid photo someone took of me from my bad side and shrug / I chew on the phrase "bad side" for a second / and spit it out / All of my daily chores feel choreographed to a beautiful piece of original music / and my chaotic multitasking is actually saving me time / I find myself content yet ambitious / calm yet flamboyant / rested but ready to pounce / I am using my curiosity for hope / my imagination for best-case scenarios / and my attention to detail for astonishment / It is 72 degrees and sunny / the wind is at my back / and the only thing I want / is everything I already have.

# Acknowledgments

I'd like to thank myself for being brave-slash-silly enough to start posting poems on the internet. That small decision shifted the course of my career in a wild way, and I'm forever indebted to me for that. Next up, is the dear soul I almost dedicated this book to: my dog, my muse: Puffin (2015–2023). He inspired many of my poems (including a very special one in this book, "I Will Remind You of Your Joy," which I wrote the week he passed away). I know he would understand that dedicating the book to Michelle Pfeiffer instead of him was simply the funnier choice. I will miss you for the rest of my life, sweet angelboy.

I'm disgustingly fortunate to have a family that I would choose again and again if it worked like that. They're each a large reason why a little girl in Minnesota always felt safe enough to be a bit much. (It's me; I'm the little girl in Minnesota.) Mom, you famously say I've been funny since I was a baby, so first and foremost let's get that in print. Thank you for showing me what unconditional love and unbridled delight look like in the wild. Emma, "Ultimate," I feel so sorry for everyone who doesn't know what it's like to be loved by you. You are loyalty embodied and remain the steadiest, funniest, fiercest presence in my life. Meredith, my very first friend, I've looked up to you for as long as I can remember, and I am so grateful to have grown up in the comforting shadow of your brilliant mind and sentimental heart. With the exception of my dance moves, you've always loved me so fully; what a gift. Jonathan, I adore you as much today as I did when you were the two-year-old I sang to sleep. You've made so much beauty from your life already and I can't wait to see what genius you cook up next.

To Jack, Davis, Selah, and Zariah: you're the most incredible little humans and you've been cracking my heart open since 2015. I'm so lucky and proud to be your Aunt Lulu.

Caleb, love of my life, you're later in this list only because you came along later. That's just science and you of all people should appreciate that. Thank you for always seeing me and celebrating me and knowing what I need before I do. Loving you is a deep breath. Dawson, technically you cowrote most of this book with me—thanks for being a week late so I could finish my copy edits. You're my sun, moon, and stars and I can't believe I get the remarkable privilege of being your mom. If I teach you one thing through my life and my work, I hope it's that amidst this wrecked world there's so much joy waiting for you. So, so much joy.

To all my friends in real life and online, thank you for not making fun of me for turning into a poet at age thirty-seven and for supporting and sharing my work with so much genuine enthusiasm. Meghan, Mike, Allie, Danny, Parker, Meggie, Nichole, Chelsey, Cassie, Amanda, Charlotte: you're the best friends a gal could ask for and true heroes for putting up with all of my antics.

This book wouldn't be possible without my whip-smart agent, Joanna MacKenzie. Thank you for sliding into my DMs when I was still a baby poet and having a vision for a book that I hadn't even had the audacity to dream up yet. Against all odds, I thoroughly enjoyed the editing process of this book and that's thanks to my editor, Sarah Cantin, who maintains an instinctive and generous vision for my work. Your insights shaped this into a collection I'm so proud to share with the world, and you've gone to bat again and again to get it in the right hands; thank you, thank you, thank you. To the rest of the team at St. Martin's—Drue and Lexi and Rebecca and Alex—thank you for using your organizational, marketing, and media prowesses to make sure everyone and their drunk cousin knows about *A Bit Much*.

This concludes my long-winded, emotional list of gratitude. Maybe in future books I'll be more concise. Probably not.

# About the Author

Hallie Duesenberg

**Lyndsay Rush** is a comedy writer, cofounder of the branding agency Obedient, and the poet behind the popular Instagram account @maryoliversdrunk cousin. Her work has been featured in *Reductress, McSweeney's, New York* magazine, and *The New York Times*. Lyndsay spent most of her adult life freezing in Chicago, but currently swelters in Nashville with her husband and young son.